Today's Joys:

Choosing Joy Every Day

by
Tania Lester

Today's Joys
Choosing Joy Every Day

by
Tania Lester

Manufactured in the United States of America

Choosing Joy

joy (noun)

1. the emotion of great delight or happiness caused by something exceptionally good or satisfying; keen pleasure; elation
2. a source or cause of keen pleasure or delight; something or someone greatly valued or appreciated:
3. the expression or display of glad feeling; festive gaiety.
4. a state of happiness or felicity.

Antonyms

1. misery, unhappiness, sorrow, grief.

Delight vs. misery, felicity vs. grief, pleasure vs. sorrow ... who wouldn't choose joy? Yet so many of us seem to spend so much of our lives mired in the depths of sorrow, lamenting those things that we think we are missing. There is a place for sorrow and grief. Some circumstances certainly warrant misery, or at the least unhappiness. But, it is an awful existence to dwell in these places. This is a collection of joy moments and stories that I hope will help others to learn how to find joy in every day, no matter your circumstances.

The Me before C

On July 26th, 2011, I was diagnosed with Stage 3-C Ovarian Cancer. Yes, this book is about finding and holding on to joy. But it is important to know the *me before C* to understand that this is not a new thing. Choosing joy has been a part of who I was before, during, and after cancer. I cannot imagine how I would have walked this path any other way. As I walked down this road, I have come upon many people whom I believe can benefit from choosing joy, if they just knew how. Many people have encouraged me to write down my journey and that is what follows. But first, let me introduce the *me before C*.

This Little Light of Mine

There are two truths that define my view of sad and happy, misery and joy, dark and light. First, white light is all the colors of light combined in the visible light spectrum. Second, darkness is the absence of light. Goodness is often portrayed as white light and badness as darkness. When I was little, I didn't like to be in the  dark. The dark is scary. A small nightlight was all it took to take away the darkness. The same is true in how we see good and bad in our lives. You see, you can make the darkness go away with just a little bit of light. But a little bit of darkness cannot take away the light. So many people live in darkness because all they see are the shadows, the bad, the things that make them unhappy. But all it takes is a little bit of light to obliterate the darkness. And, all it takes is a little bit of joy to make the hard times bearable.

Comparison & Measuring Up

> *There is so much good in the worst of us,*
> *And so much bad in the best of us,*
> *That it hardly behooves any of us*
> *To talk about the rest of us.*
> Edward Wallis Hoch (1849 - 1925)
> Marion (Kansas) Record

I came upon this poem for the first time in the 5th grade. There are many lessons to be learned from quotations and poems such as this. We are all guilty of measuring ourselves against our own perception of someone else's reality. We experience jealousy or feelings of inadequacy when we perceive that someone else seems better, or has more, or is nicer, or any number of attributes that we find short in ourselves. And, we feel sorry for others who we see as less than our own impression of ourselves. Somehow we find a way to position ourselves in a continuum between good and bad, between happy and sad, between joy and sorrow. We often allow the line that is our place on that continuum to move from one extreme to the other, and sometimes we find our place and allow ourselves to move only slightly toward one end or the other. I have come across many people who choose their place on this continuum. The saddest people I know place themselves toward the sorrow end and are continually looking for reasons to stay there. The happiest people I know do just the opposite and place themselves toward the joy end and are always finding reasons to stay in that place.

In the 5th grade, I remember lining up by height and then counting off to choose teams for kickball. I was on the shorter end of the line, sometimes at the very end. I could measure myself against the other kids and determine that in that measurement I was shorter than most. So, I could find my place. But in the happy/sad, joy/sorrow line you cannot measure yourself against anyone else. The problem is, the measures most of us use to place ourselves in any part of this line are usually external and our own perceptions of a reality that may not exist. We can never fully know the whole reality of another person's existence, circumstances, history, beliefs, internal or external struggles, or joys. Each of us is unique with our own combination of experiences, feelings, beliefs, relationships, and so many other things that make up who we are and how we see ourselves. You cannot line up on the joy meter by comparing yourself to anyone else. Where you are on that continuum is a choice. And since it is a choice, why would anyone choose to be miserable? If you want to place yourself on that continuum with a measure that has stood the test of time, consider that the word "joy" is found 242 times in the NIV Bible, and "sorrow" is only found 36 times. God wants us to lean toward the joy side of this scale.

Oh Yeah, I'll show you

When I was 14, my dad was a student at the Navy Post-graduate School in Monterey, CA. Living in the Navy housing neighborhood, I was one of the oldest children. A new family moved in down the street and I noticed there were a couple of boys who looked to be about my age. So, I started putting myself in places to watch them and hopefully meet them. When they were on their bikes, I'd don my roller skates. When they were at the playground, I'd find an excuse to walk around the trails nearby. One day these boys were playing out in the woods, so I decided to climb a tree and see what they were up to. Once I got up about 15 feet, I could see that they were catching and killing lizards. This was not something I wanted to be a part of, so I started to climb down.

The tree had several dead branches and at about the 12-foot mark, my hand found one. The branch fell and shortly afterwards, so did I, landing on my backside. A man out walking his dog saw me fall and ran up to where I was and laid me down. Pain immediately shot up and down my legs and continued until my dad made it to the woods and propped me up on his knees. The ambulance arrived about 30 minutes later and I was taken to Ft. Ord Army Hospital where it was discovered that I had crushed the 2nd lumbar vertebra. Further tests showed that the bone was split all the way around and had slipped just a little. Any further slippage would likely result in permanent spinal cord injury. I was to be kept immobilized in the hospital for nearly a month, followed by several months in a body cast and a year in a back brace.

I was very angry. Although I was not sick, I was confined to a bed on my back 24/7. I made life miserable for anyone around me. About a week into this adventure, I overheard the nurses outside my door talking to a new nurse who was just coming on shift. They described how irritable I was, how I was yelling and disturbing other people down the hall, and how they didn't know what to do other than just let me work through it.

"Oh yeah, I'll show you," I thought. At that moment, I decided to be as sweet as cream and show those nurses that they didn't have me pegged like they thought they did. Initially it was really just another form of my belligerent attitude. Glenda, the new nurse, came into my room to check on me that morning, and I smiled and talked as nicely as I could. I didn't complain about anything; instead I engaged her in conversation about a vacation from which she'd just returned. Throughout that day, she kept coming back into my room just to visit with me. The next day she brought her guitar, and we sang songs together.

Eventually, other nurses and therapists began to spend more time with me, and while I still hated that I was in that situation, I noticed that overall I felt better. I wasn't angry or bitter anymore. I had chosen to make the best of the situation, and the person who benefited the most was me. This was the first time I learned I could choose joy.

I was Glee before Glee was Cool

I started high school in a body cast. Actually, I spent the first three months of high school being home-schooled, as my body cast was bit too cumbersome for the classroom. I started high school in a brace that I wore for a year. We had just moved from Monterey, CA to Bonita, a suburb of San Diego, and we were exploring our new hometown when we had the opportunity to see "The Music Machine", Bonita Vista High School's elite show choir, perform at a local mall. Though I was still in the cast, I told my mother, "I'm going to do that." I'm not quite sure she believed me. I signed up for voice lessons and as soon as my doctor cleared it, I started taking dance lessons.

Though I had always had an affinity for music, I never had a great talent. But I did have a strong desire and once I'd made up my mind I was determined. I signed up for the concert choir as soon as I was able to actually go to school. The next year, I auditioned for and made it into the all-girls *Sound Unlimited* show choir, one step below *Music Machine*. But I still had my sights set on the Machine.

Getting into the group was extremely competitive. The group was made up of 12 boys and 12 girls and there were a number of returning members, which further limited my chances. In the spring of my junior year, I started the audition process, which included vocal auditions and dance auditions. My voice was just okay. I could carry a tune, but I did not have a strong or powerful voice. My back injury had left me with nerve damage and weakness, which made dancing challenging. I took lessons three times a week and practiced every chance I got. When it came time for the audition, I put every ounce of my heart and soul into my performance. I made it into the group as an alternate and had to defend my position in the fall, which I did. My year in the Music Machine and the years of preparation leading up to it definitely helped make me who I am today. I was a part of something bigger than me. I proved to myself that perseverance pays off.

Mommy, I'm a Magician

When my son was four or five-years-old he fell in love with magic. He loved wearing a magician's cape and hat, and carried a magic wand around with him to cast spells. One night he brought me a ball and a blanket and said, "Mommy I'm a magician and I'm going to make  this ball disappear." He handed me the ball and then covered it with his blanket. He waved his wand around and chanted, "Abracadabra, disappear ball." I discretely dropped the ball between my legs and when he removed the blanket it was nowhere to be seen. I feigned disbelief, and though he was a bit shocked he was completely convinced that he had actually performed magic. I said, "Can you make it come back?" "Sure, I can," he said. So he placed the blanket over my hands and waved the wand and chanted, "Abracadabra, come back ball." When he removed the blanket, the ball was back in my hand. We did the trick over and over for at least an hour. We showed his sisters and dad and, while they all knew that it was a trick, everyone made a huge deal about Cody's talent.

Some may think it was mean of me to fool my five-year-old son. But that night gave him confidence in himself that I had never before seen. He eventually figured out that he had not actually made the ball disappear, but by that time he had used his confidence to build more confidence. He wasn't angry.

I think God works the same way. As a parent, we have a broader perspective of the world than our children do. Therefore, we are able to understand how things work and use that knowledge to help our children learn and grow. If we can do that for our children, just imagine what an all-knowing, omnipotent God can do for us. We believe we make our own magic. But just as I helped Cody make the ball disappear, God helps us make our own joy.

Finding the Joy Moments

When each of my daughters went away to college, they would often call home with myriad complaints, which consisted of the absolute worst things that could have happened in their whole lives. Things such as: a bad grade, or a difficult class; roommates who would not be quiet, or clean up after themselves; walking to class through the rain; missing class because they didn't feel well. All sorts of excuses to steal their joy. My response was always, "Find your joy moment in today and hold on to it." Sometimes I would talk them through finding their joy moment, such as going outside and looking up at the sky and finding a picture in the clouds that made them smile. Find a bud for a flower about to bloom and thank God for the promise of spring. Seek out a friend and talk about nothing.

Joy moments don't have to be big. They don't have to announce themselves as the answer to all your prayers, hopes, or wishes. And they don't have to measure up to whatever is not good in your life. A joy moment can be a shiny grain of sand in an hourglass of sorrows. It is sometimes hard to find the shiny grain amidst the grey and dreary. But, once you find it and hold on to it, it will brighten that moment and lighten your heart. And the next joy moment will be easier to find.

My son is dyslexic. He perceives his world differently than the rest of us *normal* people. I have always considered his dyslexia as a gift rather than applying a label of learning disability. A dyslexic brain sees more of the world than the rest of us. They can see every grain of sand from the top, the bottom, side-to-side, forwards and backwards, and they get to choose which way to interpret what they see. We used to play "I Spy" puzzles and Cody would always find whatever it was we were searching for first. Because he sees more of his world, he has more choices to make about how he interprets his world. This is why dyslexic people have trouble learning to read. Where you and I would see the word CAT and have a choice to read it as CAT or TAC, Cody sees at least seven other options and has to choose between nine choices instead of two. But this also gives him an opportunity to find more of those grains of shiny sand. He finds more joy moments because he has more sand to sift through, and he has learned to choose joy.

The Joy Box

Several years ago, as I was trying to figure out the perfect Christmas gifts for everyone in my family, I realized that everyone already had everything they really wanted or needed and any gift that I gave would have little meaning. *Things* were not important. Their toy boxes were already overflowing. Plus, we didn't have a lot of extra money that season and as I was traveling for work, I didn't have a lot of time to shop for just the perfect trinket. One night while alone in a hotel room in Palo Alto, California, it occurred to me that nobody in my family needed any more toys. So, I decided to give *joys* instead of *toys*. When I got home, I went to a local craft store and bought simple balsa wood boxes of different sizes and shapes, along with some paints and glitter. I spent a total of $3.00 per person and made everyone a *Joy Box*. I wrote the following poem and put inside each joy box:

When times are good
When times are bad
When you're happy
If you're sad

No matter what
God finds a way
To give you joy
In every day

A ray of sunshine
A drop of rain
A simple smile
To ease your pain

Open this box
When you feel down
Reflect on Joy
You've already found

And on those days
When joys are many
Add to this box
Of Joys-A-Plenty

This Joy Box
Was made for you
Because you're my joy
And I love you

And then I set about collecting joys. There were over 100 packages under the tree that year, but most of them contained only a *Joy Card,* with a reminder of a joy the recipient had received that year. By the time all the packages were opened, the joy boxes were full of cards and the room was full of smiles. Every one of my children said it was the best Christmas ever.

I had made a joy box for everyone except me. So, the next year my husband built me a Joy Box that is 18" square (their boxes were the size of small jewelry boxes) and said that he knew I would have it full before the end of the next year. Each year since then, we have done something different with Joy Cards. Some joy cards have been used to remember favorite Christmas memories, others to say Thank You to family members who have touched us throughout the year. But no matter how the joy cards are used, sitting around our Christmas tree for the past several years is no longer about the gluttony of presents, but the presence of joy.

Freedom to make mistakes

For more than fifteen years, I have held management positions, leading anywhere from three to sixty people at any given time. I enjoy managing teams of people because I love helping them to grow and become more than they thought they could be. I held several management philosophies that I would share with any new team members. The first was that it was my job to stand in front of them when they were failing and behind them when they succeeded, and that I preferred the view from the back. Another was that if you weren't making a mistake, you weren't trying hard enough. These philosophies gave my employees the freedom to do their jobs to the best of their abilities without always second guessing themselves or worrying about getting into trouble.

This is how I approach life as well. God allows me to feel happy when things go well, and holds me up when they don't. He allows me to make mistakes and forgives me no matter what. Because of this, I have never been a worrier. It drives my husband crazy because he wants to know what is going to happen next. He wants to plan for the next step, the next phase, retirement, whatever. And while I know it is important to prepare, I cannot stress about those things. I didn't know ten years ago where I would be today or how I would get here. I don't know where I will be in five years, or even tomorrow, or what will happen between now and then. But, I do know that God will provide. I know there will be hard times and there will be easy times. There will be moments of sorrow and moments of joy. God sets our path for us, and he laughs at us when we try to navigate ourselves.

As I look back on my life I can see the stepping stones of joy that got me to where I am today, but I cannot see the path ahead. I can also see the moments of pain and sorrow, but those are not the ones that shaped who I have become. Some of them I believe were God's nudging to get me back on the right path. Some of them were things I cannot begin to understand, such as my baby sister dying in a car crash at the age of 17, or my daughter losing her hearing at age 2 due to meningitis. I know many people who have chosen to hang on to their sorrows like a weighty charm necklace. While I don't understand why these things happened, I recognize that out of even the hardest things there were joys to be found. My baby sister was a joyful, happy child. She showed her world how to laugh and that is a joy I have on my charm necklace. My daughter sings like an angel, even though she has no hearing in one ear and only 80% hearing in the other. I have many hours of listening to her music on my joy necklace. These would both have been joyful without the accompanying sorrow, but they are made more meaningful because of it.

My "Testimony"

I am the granddaughter of a minister and the daughter of a PK (preacher's kid). Most PKs are either really good or not. My mother falls into the first category. She never swears, only drinks sparingly, will do anything for anyone, sometimes to her own demise, and is generally who I think of when I think of someone who is a really good person. She was raised in the Methodist church, literally. In his youth, my father went to church two to three times a week and even attended a Christian college for a year before joining the Navy. Whether it was a conscious decision or not, my parents did not "church" me or my sisters as we were growing up. I remember church as a place we went primarily when we visited grandparents, and my most vivid memories of church involved a lot of standing-up, sitting-down, and paste.

My grandfather gave me "The Children's Bible" when I was about 11-years-old. As an avid reader, I read it from cover to cover twice. So, I felt knowledgeable about the stories of the bible. I thought that most of the people I knew *believed* in God and were *good* people. I also came to learn that there were a lot of fundamentalist Christians who were either so *needy* that they couldn't take care of themselves without leaning on the crutch of Christ, or were so self-righteous that only God Himself could measure up to their ideal of who a good Christian should be.

Though I worked in a church for several years in my 20s, I never saw the need to align myself to either of the "sides" of Christianity as I saw it. I was perfectly capable of taking care of myself. I believed there was a God, but other people needed him more than I did. So, I sacrificially let them have Him. In my mid-thirties, my middle daughter announced that we *should* go to church, and so we did. We began attending a seeker-sensitive, non-denominational church with some friends. For almost a year (though we faithfully attended every week) I held to my assertion that letting go and letting God, or leaning on the crutch of Christ was something other people needed. I liked the music and the message, but beyond that I was fine as I was. I had read or heard stories of people finding God in their darkest moments. But I was not in a dark place. In fact, all was right in my world. I was in a good place at work, my marriage was great, and my kids were happy and healthy. But I began to feel as if something was missing. I fought it for a long time. I didn't need anything. I was fully capable of making my own way and I was doing just fine. I really was.

Many of the stories I had heard of other people accepting Jesus as their savior involved falling on their knees and confessing that they just couldn't make it without Him. The ripping of the shroud or the curtain seemed like such a drastic and violent event. It didn't happen like that for me. It was more like a light tapping on the door, or maybe the silence that happens as the lights go down and the curtain rises before a grand performance begins. It was quiet. It was a nudging. God just kept whispering to me ... "there's more if you want it" ... "I'm here" ... "All you need to do is open the door and let me in" ... "perhaps you can do it all on your own, but you don't have to" ... and finally just before Christmas about fifteen years ago, I cracked open that door—I watched the lights go down and experienced the most exquisite music and the brightest of lights and my world changed forever.

There was a change in the way I felt. I had always been a mostly positive person. I had always been a mostly happy person. But suddenly I was a lighter person. A weight that I didn't even know I was carrying was lifted from my shoulders. I didn't tell anyone about my *transformation* for several days. I wanted to make sure I wasn't going crazy, or that it wasn't just a silly phase. But it became real for me when a co-worker noticed I was a different person.

I thought I was going about my life the same as I always had. I went to work, conducted sometimes contentious meetings, came home, made dinner, checked homework, watched some TV, snuck in a little Bible reading on the side (okay, that part was new), and went to bed. One day after a particularly difficult meeting, a co-worker confronted me and said, "What's wrong with you?" Apparently, I had not conducted myself quite as strongly or forcefully as she had expected. In fact, I had been letting things happen that I never before would have allowed. I didn't try to control events as I would have in the past. And in the end, the results were significantly better than they might have been if I had tried to control them. The funny thing was that I did not feel like I had to control it. I let go and let God. And my co-worker noticed. It scared her. She thought I'd lost my edge. Even though things had been going well, they got better. And I knew that I didn't do it. I knew that I had just let go and suddenly things worked better than they had before. So, what's wrong, she asked? I answered her by telling her what was right. I told her that I had made some changes in my life and my outlook and that I wasn't in control, never really had been, and that God was steering my ship now. She looked at me as if I had lost my mind. I smiled and told her that I hoped one day she would be as free as I was and would know what I was feeling. I have lost touch with that co-worker, so I don't know what's become of her. But, I think God may have planted a seed that day and I hope she has found the peace that transcends all understanding.

My testimony is not a *falling on my face in anguish* and begging for God. It was a gentle handing over of the reigns. I will not pretend that life has been a bed of roses ever since that moment, or that I do not have my share of trials and struggles and sorrows. I will say that when I do not try to lift my burdens on my own, I find that they are much lighter. When I listen to the nudging and gentle guidance of God, my path is made clear. I have experienced many miracles, some big and some small—but I know that God works in my life and that when I listen I am better for it. He shows me His joy and light all the time. It is always there.

Playing Piano for a Celebrity

I don't remember how long ago, so I guess it's been a while, my church held our annual Women's Retreat and invited Ellie Lafaro as our guest speaker. Ellie had just published her book "Bonding with the Blonde Women", which described her brunette, Italian, Ellie move from Brooklyn to Reston, Virginia, and her adventures getting to know the stay-at-home PTA *blonde* moms in her neighborhood. Unbeknownst to the retreating ladies, about 25 of us, she brought her dear friend Kathy Troccoli. Once we noticed that a star was among us, Ellie let it be known that Kathy was not there as a Christian Singer, or a star, or to be treated any differently than anyone else. She was there to retreat along with us. It didn't take long for Kathy to be one of the girls, though secretly we were all star-struck.

I was providing most of the music for the weekend, playing keyboards for our worship time as well as playing quietly as Ellie closed each session with prayer. At the end of the last session, just as Ellie began to pray and I was playing quietly, Kathy snuck up behind me and asked if I knew *Shout To The Lord*. I quickly thumbed through my book with my left hand while I continued to play with my right hand, until I found the chord chart. She looked at it and then said, "Um, can you play it in 'A'?" So, I started transposing in my head and writing (again with my left hand and I am right-handed) new chords on the sheet and then put it up on the stand. Ellie was watching out of the corner of her eye to be sure we were ready as she finished praying. Just as she said "Amen", I started playing the song and Kathy started singing right over my shoulder. The ladies opened their eyes in amazement and sang along. My friend later told me that I was white as a ghost. It is a moment I'll never forget.

I have had the opportunity to see Ellie and Kathy many times over the past several years at their "An Evening In December" concerts held in local churches. Sometimes I get an opportunity to speak to them afterwards. Five days after my fifth chemo treatment, I convinced my loving husband to take me to their concert. He was the only man among what seemed like 1000 women who enjoyed a wonderful evening of Christmas Carols and Kathy's new song, "I'll Be Missing You This Christmas", belly laughs from Ellie's dry humor, and tears from her touching message. But the best part came when I got a hug from my "old friend" Kathy after the concert.

A Curse and a Blessing All-In-One

The joy in the next several stories may not be as evident as others, but they serve to set the stage for one of the hardest things I've ever had to face. If I had not known how to choose joy, I don't know how I would have been able to cope. It is my hope that this book reaches many people no matter their circumstances. This section describes my journey through Ovarian Cancer, and it is my greatest hope that my words can help anyone else who may have or will be touched by the "C" word or any other life threatening illness. I include my personal experience throughout this journey, including diagnosis, surgery, pathology, and chemo-therapy and its side effects. Part of my motivation for writing this is to help other cancer survivors and their care-givers to better understand what to expect and how I learned to cope and find the joy. The stories in "The Me Before C" hopefully show that I already knew how to choose joy, but this experience has helped to make joy a permanent part of every day of my life.

Starting down a new road

On Sunday July 24th, my middle daughter told me that she would disown me if I didn't go to the doctor and get an inhaler for a nagging cough that had been plaguing me for three or four months. Several days before that, I had noticed a small *lump* in my lower abdomen. In the preceding six months, I had lost over 30 pounds and I determined that possibly that lump had been there all along and without the extra insulation I was just noticing it. I also thought, after looking up some sites on the Internet, that it might be an ovarian cyst—and the prescription for that was to wait through a cycle and it would likely go away.

I wasn't worried, but on Monday the 25th I discovered that my calendar was fairly light and so I decided to call Dr. P and see if I could make an appointment. He could see me at 11:30 that morning, so after stopping in at my office for a few hours I went to Dr. P's office where I filled out a "What's Going On" form. The first thing I noted was the cough and then decided to add to the bottom of the form that I had noticed a small lump. Dr. P spent about fifteen minutes diagnosing the source of the cough and finally determined that I was likely allergic to my daughter's pet rabbit. He prescribed an inhaler, which I didn't plan to use because I just don't like those things. He then went on to check out the lump.

As soon as he began probing my abdomen, I knew that the cough was not going to be an issue anymore. I was about to have to deal with something much more serious. He took my hand and had me feel several other areas of my midsection and then said he'd like to run a CT scan to see what was going on, and that he was concerned my colon might be affected. I called my husband, and began working with the imaging center to get scheduled for a CT scan that afternoon.

Within about fifteen minutes of arriving home after the scan, Dr. P called to tell me that it wasn't my colon, but it was my ovary and he wanted to schedule me with a surgeon the next day. My first reaction was—that's great, because at 46 years old, with three grown children and two grandchildren, I didn't really need my ovaries anymore, but I was sort of attached to my colon. Dr. P laughed and said I had a great attitude and he would call me the next morning with an appointment time with the surgeon.

I didn't really think about my attitude. I didn't stress at all about what might be going on. I didn't research anything on the Internet. I determined to go on with whatever the next steps were to be. My son was due to arrive that night, home on leave from the Navy, and he'd already made plans to go with my husband to visit my father-in-law about three hours away the next day. So, I decided that since we didn't really know what was going on yet, we should just go on with the plans as they were. I called my sister, a veteran of several medical issues involving both the colon and lady parts, and she agreed to go with me to see the surgeon the next day. It didn't even occur to me that the surgeon I would be seeing was also an oncologist. As fast as it happened, I took baby steps into the world of cancer.

Talking to the tumor

On July 26th my sister and I met with a wonderful man who has assisted God in saving my life. The appointment began with his reading through the CT report, which I could barely read upside down on his desk. I followed along with what he was saying as best I could—though the language was not one that I spoke—but my eye was drawn to the bottom of the report where I could make out the words, "Likely Ovarian Cancer". That was the first moment I considered the "C" word. After that, he led us to an exam room and as I was changing clothes I asked my sister if she could see the bottom of the report. She had not seen it and I told her that the "C" word was on it and she said, "Well, if it is—then we'll deal with it." She had been thinking about that all along. After my phone call the night before, she had done some research and had prepared a full-page list of questions. She already knew what I hadn't even imagined.

Dr. K came back into the room and started his exam— from head-to-toe. As he was listening to my heart he said, "Hmm, a little fast," and then he leaned down closer, smiled, and said, "Our nurses sometimes have that effect on people." Then as he got to my abdomen he began to talk to what I would later learn was a 5-lb cantaloupe-sized tumor. He said, "Ah ha, and who are you? You do not belong here. We're going to have to take care of you. We're going to get you out of there." All in all, it was the most physically uncomfortable, yet the best, exam I had ever had. I was so comforted by this man.

After the physical exam, we went back into his office where he brought up the CT scan on his computer and proceeded to introduce us to the tumor that was invading my mid-section. He described a 21-cm ovarian tumor along with at least three enlarged (by 300%) lymph nodes. It was also apparent that the other ovary may have been affected. And that little lump I felt was my uterus being pushed out of place by this invader. As he described all of these things, he took a piece of paper with a pen & ink drawing of the reproductive system. With the picture facing toward me, he proceeded to write upside-down "The Problem" and "What we will do about it". He then listed ovarian tumor, enlarged lymph nodes and eventually "Stage 3-C Ovarian Cancer". Under what we will do about it, he listed full hysterectomy, lymph node removal, and chemo-therapy—6-8 courses. My first question was "the hair-falling out kind?" I didn't know what stage 3-C meant. I knew it was worse than 2, but not as bad as 4. But, my first thought was about my hair. He then said that we should do the surgery within 2-3 weeks and proceeded to thumb through his appointment book to find a date. He said he was available two weeks later and would pencil me in. I started thinking about my kids and remembering that my son was only home for a little over a week, and I didn't know if he could get leave again so soon. I wondered aloud if he should be there or not and I started spinning. Dr. K looked at his book again and said he could probably "squeeze me in" that Saturday, but I'd have to let him know first thing in the morning. That seemed too soon. There was so much to process. I was in shock.

The Silent Killer or Teal is the Color

Both my mother and my sister are breast cancer survivors. Both of them were diagnosed early and are survivors thanks to lumpectomies and radiation. This, I believe, is because there is a huge movement through the Susan B. Komen foundation for  Breast Cancer awareness. Mammograms and self-exams have saved the lives of so many women because they knew to do it. I also lost a very dear friend to breast cancer. She was in her mid-thirties when she was initially diagnosed and had never had a mammogram. She lost her battle in a recurrence that appeared as bone cancer and moved into other organs before taking her life, before she was able to see her children grow up. Early screening may have saved her, but we'll never know. At least there are routine tests and screening and awareness for breast cancer now.

Ovarian cancer on the other hand is a silent killer. The symptoms for Ovarian Cancer are easily dismissed and easily misdiagnosed. These symptoms include bloating, frequent urination, loss of appetite, unexplained weight loss (or gain), and fatigue. Ok, I'm 46 years old, have had three children, work full-time, have two grandchildren, and live in a major metropolitan area, living a fairly fast-paced life. Who wouldn't expect to experience bloating, frequent urination (had 3 kids and getting older), loss of appetite—okay, I thought I was doing that on my own as my husband and I had embarked on a weight loss effort and I had decided mind over matter (or food) was working—and the fatigue I chalked up to my lifestyle and the fact that we had started exercising (walking and biking). None of these symptoms, though evident for a long time, pointed to a cancer diagnosis, because I didn't know they should. I am one of the fortunate ones who had a wonderful doctor who knew what to look for and didn't waste any time determining an accurate diagnosis. I was also referred to one of the few doctors in the world who is an oncologist, gynecologist, and surgeon all in one. All the pieces lined up perfectly to put me in the right place, at the right time, with the right doctors. But, if I had paid attention to these symptoms or if I had not put off my annual physicals (it had been three years since I actually went to my annual physical) then my cancer may not have mutated to where it did, if at all.

My cancer turned out to be a mutated endometriosis that could have happened a year ago, three years ago, or even ten years ago. But, being the strong woman that I am, I ignored it and pushed through it. I didn't even know what endometriosis was. Nothing I could do about it anyway, so just get past it. I do not say this to second-guess or wish-I-had. I write this now to encourage all the women who read this to pay attention to your bodies. Don't put off your annual appointments with your doctors. Trust me, I have more than made up for all the hours I saved not going to the doctor, as I have visited at least one doctor every week for nearly six months, so far. Pay attention to your body and tell your doctor about any symptoms you may be experiencing, no matter how silly it might sound. Be your own advocate and if something doesn't feel right, find out why; don't push through it. Since my diagnosis, I have delivered this message to all my lady friends and I have encouraged all my man friends or acquaintances to tell their lady friends. In the last six months I am aware of at least ten women in my world who have made appointments and seen their doctors, who probably would not have. Some have resulted in further treatment for various ailments, others are perfectly healthy. At least ten women that I know of will not let this silent killer sneak up on them and for that I am grateful.

One of the motivations for writing this book is part of my outreach to other women to get the word out. If one life is saved, then my joy is found. Most diagnoses for ovarian cancer are found in later stages, but that doesn't have to be the case. There are early warning signs. There is a screening blood-test, ultrasounds, CT scans, and other exams that can diagnose this disease before it reaches the life-threatening stages. And with more education and awareness, we can increase the early diagnosis and subsequent survival from ovarian cancer.

I would venture to say there is not a woman in the United States who doesn't know about breast cancer and what to look for. October is Breast Cancer Awareness and Pink is the color. I was amazed at the flood of pink and all the awareness campaigns that are out there. Well, Teal is the color for Ovarian Cancer and September is Ovarian Cancer Awareness month. It is my hope that one day we will see as much teal as we do pink and that women will receive regular screening. And that just as we are seeing a much higher survival rate in breast cancer, we will see the same in Ovarian Cancer.

How to tell my family

Receiving a diagnosis for Ovarian Cancer was not the hardest part of July the 26th. Telling my family was. My sister took me home where my 22-year-old daughter was sitting in the family room watching TV. My husband and 20-year-old son were on their way home from my father-in-law's house three hours away. My 25-year-old daughter lives four hours away and my parents are eleven hours away. Does one just pick up the phone and say, "Hey, guess what happened today?" The first call I made was to my pastor. I knew I was going to need strength that I didn't have all by myself. My pastor has been a part of my family's lives for over fifteen years. He has laughed with us, he has cried with us, he married my daughter, and most importantly he has prayed with us and for us.

My parents were due to arrive at my house later in the week to visit with my son who was home on leave from the Navy. My sister and I called them together and I told my mother that she might want to pack a larger suitcase, because I might need her to stay a little longer than they were expecting. I am so grateful for my sister that day. She was able to tell my parents what was happening without alarming them too much. We still didn't really know what was going to happen, what the diagnosis really meant, or what help we would need. I think there were some fear tears, but mainly we just started making plans.

The next part was telling my children and my husband. These are the people who rely on me to be the strong one and on this day, that wasn't me. I made the decision to tell them everything I knew. I wasn't going to sugar-coat anything. I needed them to know everything I knew so that I could lean on them. My sister, brother-in-law and I went downstairs where my 22-year-old was and I asked her to turn off the TV and sit with me for a minute. I don't know what words I used, but I told her that I had been to the doctor and that he had found something they thought was cancer and that he was going to remove it as soon as we could. She burst into tears and after holding each other and crying for a while, she said, "So, this is what this feels like." Her reaction was so raw and so genuine. I had developed a good adult relationship with all my children over the years, but in that moment a new bond was forged between Kacie and me. One of her friends' families is also living with cancer, and her friend was the one who told her that it would be the *greatest curse and blessing* all-in-one that our family would ever experience. That has certainly proven to be true.

Next was the phone call to my oldest daughter. I knew she was at a bible study at her church in southern Virginia. So, I sent her a text message and told her to give me a call when she got home. It was important that she be at home with her husband when I told her. She called from church before she went home. Somehow, I held it together enough to encourage her to go on home and call me there. I know she knew something bad had happened, but she trusted me enough to know that she needed to be home before I told her. She called back as soon as she got home and after I shared the news with her, she and her sister were able to talk to and encourage each other. It was like a foundation was being forged to bear the weight of what was to come. Each person was another part of that foundation and they each came together and held each other up and together they all held me up. My pastor arrived shortly after that and then my husband and son got home.

Telling my son was the hardest. He is the baby in the family and had been through so much, enlisting in the Navy, and he had been home less than 24 hours. Again, after telling him, he and his sisters held each other up. I didn't get to tell my husband by himself. He learned the news as I told my son. I am so grateful that my pastor was there because he was able to pray with my husband right there and then and there was peace. We knew that this was not something that any of us could handle, control, or manage on our own. A transformation occurred in that room and in my family that night. It was the beginning of the blessing. Nothing else mattered in that moment. We were together, some virtually on the phone, and we were going to be all right because we had already begun to lean on each other in a way we never before had. There has always been a lot of love in my family, but just like the Grinch whose heart grew three sizes when he heard the Whos singing—the love in my family grew that night in ways we never knew could happen.

What to do next

My brother-in-law, having heard that surgery the next Saturday was an option vs. waiting two weeks, strongly encouraged me to just do it. Get it done as soon as possible. I was really torn. I felt like there was so much I needed to do to get ready for this new adventure. But finally he and everyone else convinced me there was no need to wait. So the next morning I called the doctor's office and asked if Saturday was still an option. As it turned out, while Dr. K could do the surgery on Saturday, the hospital couldn't. So, my doctor changed his vacation schedule to enable him to perform the surgery the following Tuesday.

The days leading up to the surgery were hard too. My parents and my daughter and her family arrived. I was able to spend time with everyone. But one of the hardest things was that several people wanted or needed me to make them feel better. They wanted reassurance from me. And, I didn't have it to give. I didn't know what would happen. I didn't have the strength or will to fake it. But, we could talk about it and that's what we did. I talked about how I felt. They talked about how they felt and we prayed a lot.

My Inner Circle of Prayer Warriors

Now that I am putting all of this in a book, it is strange to remember that I wanted this all kept as a close-held secret. Even that first night, my pastor wanted to alert the prayer chain and start getting people from church to surround me. I had told my boss, but refused to tell anyone else that I worked with. In those first few days, fewer than ten people knew what had happened—or was about to happen. Within a few days, I broadened that circle to about 25 people, including some of my work and church friends in what I called my "Inner Circle of Prayer Warriors". I swore them all to secrecy. I didn't want to be the subject of hallway gossip at work and I didn't want emails flying around nor did I want any pity. I chose people who I knew to be strong pray-ers and who I knew I could trust to keep my secret.

Several people suggested that I start one of the websites where people could be kept up-to-date and post well wishes as I traveled this road. But I would have nothing to do with any of that. This also meant that the people I let into my circle had to lean on each other and could not reach out to their inner circles. It wasn't until several weeks later, when I finally let the word out (on Facebook) that I realized just how selfish I had been. My children had had to bear this mainly among themselves. My family could rely on each other, but they couldn't reach out to others to gain additional strength, and I had tried to stop the people who care about me from reaching out and caring about me. One of the greatest things I have learned and one of my greatest joys is that people want to help and by letting them I was helping them. Simply allowing someone to bring a meal, or send a card, or chocolate-covered-strawberries, or stop by just to visit, or run an errand were things I didn't want to need. But my Inner Circle of Prayer Warriors and their Inner Circles and the ripples of circles needed to be allowed to help me. One of the ways I choose joy is by helping others. I did not want to be the one being helped. It was my dad who finally convinced me I was doing a disservice to those who loved me by not letting them do what they needed to do for me. I have been so blessed by so many people, some I didn't even know, who have reached out in so many ways. I received phone calls from far away friends, visits with neighbors, my porch decorated for Halloween, so many smiles and hugs. My inner circle of prayer warriors is more than 300 strong, spanning nearly the entire US and as many as 7 other countries—and that's just the ones I know by name.

Mother Theresa was once quoted saying "God doesn't give you more than you can handle, I just wish he didn't trust me so much." Throughout this journey there were many times that I wished he didn't trust me so much. One lesson that I learned is that He doesn't expect you to carry any burden by yourself. When Moses arms became too weary to hold them up any longer, Aaron came along side and held up Moses arms for him. In the same way I had a wonderful group of friends and family from near and far come and hold me up.

You and I met for a reason, and it wasn't golf

"You sure do get a lot of swing for your buck," said an admiral with whom I was *playing* golf—during an office captain's ball golf outing—about twenty years ago. When I was a teenager, my dad taught me the basics of golf. I generally know which club to use, I can usually hit the ball the first time, and I play the *cart-path-rule*. The cart-path-rule is to aim for the cart path because if the ball gets a good bounce, it might make it at least toward the hole. Over the last twenty years, I have played less than ten times, and not very well. As we were fast approaching the "empty nest", I had decided golf would be a good pastime for me and my husband. And, if I was going to play, I wanted to learn how to do it correctly. Five days before my diagnosis, I had my first golf lesson with Cathy.

We hit it off right away, figuratively and literally. With just a few pointers, I was hitting a 7 iron better than I ever thought I could. My next lesson was scheduled for the day of my surgery, so I emailed Cathy and told her I would not be able to make it to that lesson. Though I didn't know why, I also, uncharacteristically, told her why.

A day or so later, I received an email from Cathy. She told me that she was a 7-year cancer survivor and that if I wanted to talk, just reach out. So, I did.

Throughout this journey, we've met for "coffee"—lasting several hours—at least once between each chemo treatment. And, we've become friends. Just before Christmas and my last treatment Cathy wrote me an email saying, "You and I met for a reason, and it wasn't golf." I'm looking forward to growing my friendship with Cathy—and learning to play golf.

I have met many new friends throughout this journey. I've met women who are long-time cancer survivors and some who are just venturing into the journey. Cancer gives one the freedom to be vulnerable. While I would never wish a cancer diagnosis on anyone, I have made more genuine friends in the last six months than I have in the last six years—maybe longer.

I Will Do 100% of What I Can to Fix This

When my daughter was diagnosed with spinal meningitis at age 2, my husband asked the doctor what the chances were for her survival. I literally hit him. In my mind, her not surviving was not even an option and we were not going to consider it as a possibility. We were going to do whatever we had to do to make her better. One of the differences between me and my husband is that he tends to explore the possibilities—all of the possibilities—and think or talk about them all. He sometimes says that I am an ostrich with my head in the sand, or that I see the world through rose-colored glasses. That's not true. I know that bad things happen. I know everything doesn't always work out. Much of what you've read of my life so far proves that. But, I don't make them a possibility that I need to process until it happens. Someone once told me that worry is interest paid on trouble not yet due. With that mindset, I determined this cancer thing was all fixable. It wasn't going to be fun, but it was going to be fixed.

My daughter was with me for my pre-op appointment with Dr. K. After he went through all the things he planned to do (including a full hysterectomy, removing suspicious lymph nodes, possible colon resection, biopsies, chemo, and scans), my daughter said, "My mom believes that this is 100% fixable, but I want hear that from you." Dr. K replied, "I will do 100% of what I can to fix this." That was good enough for me and for her. I trusted this man and I knew he would keep his word. By the way, as I write this, Dr. K has told me four times so far that I am cancer-free. So—he kept his word.

Statistics and What They Don't Mean

During that first appointment, Dr. K gave us some literature about the diagnosis. There were books and pamphlets and lists of websites. One night early in the journey, I decided to thumb through one of the books and I found the definition for the various stages; I, II, III, IV and A, B, C. I learned that stage III-C, which was my diagnosis at that time, meant that the cancer was likely in multiple organs (both ovaries counted) and in the lymphatic system. It was also the highest you could get before Stage IV. Okay, I could deal with that because I still believed it was all fixable. But then I stumbled upon a page with survival statistics. I won't recount those statistics now because I don't want to shock anyone the way that I was shocked. Suffice it to say I lost it. I called my sister and said, "You have to talk me down from this."

I had learned that most ovarian cancers were found in the later stages, and I had learned that most diagnoses were in post-menopausal women over 60 who had never had children. So, I'd already beaten that statistic—I was in my 40's, had not even started menopause, and had delivered 3 children. So...if I beat that statistic, I could beat the others. I had a dear aunt who passed away this fall at the age of 94 who would never tell anyone how old she was. I would be in a lot of trouble if she knew I had published her age. She said, "Age is just a number and mine is unlisted." My pastor said, "The statistics for raising people from the dead are not that great, but God did it—twice." Statistics are just numbers and they are based on limited information that changes as new advances are made, and they are not about any one person. Every statistic is about history and it changes even before it is published. Everyone's story is different. From that moment on, I vowed to avoid all statistics.

The Joy Book...Today's Joys...

My daughters are both very creative and enjoy different arts and crafts type projects. So, I asked my middle daughter to make me a "Joy Book". It was my intention to journal my experience, and I wanted her to have something tangible to work on. She bought a journal and proceeded to decorate it with all manner of stickers and flowers and she wrote encouraging words in it. For the first several weeks, I used that Joy Book to write down the joys I found. Some days it was incredibly hard to find a joy. Some days it still is. But I tried to find something every day. Some of the joys that I've recorded are found in stories in this book. Some are huge miracles. And some are as simple as tasting a piece of candy, or catching a glimpse of sunlight in a cloudy, rainy sky.

Once I let the secret out, the joy book was put on a shelf and I began writing "Today's Joys ..." as my status on my Facebook page. I don't post joys every day. Not because I don't find them, but some days it's just too hard to get on the computer and post them. One day shortly after surgery, I allowed myself to have a "Feel Sorry for Myself Day". I spent most of the day on the couch watching reruns of an awful old TV show. I had decided that I deserved to feel sorry for myself. That night I posted as my Facebook status: "I am having a hard time finding my joys today, so I'm reaching out to my friends to share their joys." I received over 20 responses within the first hour ... with things like: got in and out of the grocery store in less than 30 minutes ... pink clouds ... planning a camping trip with the boy scouts ...a phone call from a friend ... finishing a project for work at 2:30 in the morning, but at least getting to sleep some ... having a beer—(ok that one was from my 20-year-old nephew ... uh huh) ... cleaning out the garage. One person told a story about a friend who had gone into a changing room to try on a new outfit and when she came out to check the mirror she realized she had forgotten to put her pants back on ... not a joy for her, but funny. Several of my friends named me as their joy for the day. So there I was feeling sorry for myself and yet there really were real joys to be had and several people in my world thought I was one of them. As I read those joys, I realized just how miserable I had felt all day—physically, emotionally, and mentally. Feeling sorry for myself did not make me feel better at all. I have not allowed myself to have a day like that since then. It's still sometimes hard to find the joy and sometimes I still reach out to others to share theirs, and they do. And it just proves that even when they're hard to find—there is joy in every day.

Those joy moments and "Today's Joys" are what prompted several of my friends to encourage me to write this book. I have gone back through my Facebook posts of the past six months and it's amazing what I've noted. There are hundreds, maybe thousands, of different joys. Spending time with friends, a taste, Ambien, a meaningful scripture, a song, a hug, driving a car, riding in a car, a warm blanket, a cool washcloth, fried pickles ... the list is endless. As I've said before, joys don't have to be big. They don't have to be the answer to a prayer or hope or wish. They don't have to measure up to the hardships you may be facing. But, it is choosing to look for them and hold on to them instead of the hardship that works. I have had many physically or emotionally or mentally hard days in the past six months. But none were as bad as the day I decided to feel sorry for myself. And all it took to stop that was to find some joys. Today's joys included writing this passage.

Dressed for the Occasion

 Preparing for surgery was like preparing for a trip when you don't know where you're going, how you're getting there, or worse what to wear. When we met with Dr. K to talk about the upcoming surgery, he described every detail including exactly what turns to take upon arriving at the hospital. He described my walk down the hallway, where to find the receptionist, and what to do once I reached my pre-op cubicle, including donning a beautiful blue and white polka-dot gown. "And once you are dressed for the occasion, I will be in to see you and make sure we're ready to go," he said. My daughter was with me for that appointment she just loved that "dressed for the occasion" phrase. It was especially fun with Dr. K's German accent – you can imagine. The night before surgery, both of my daughters disappeared. Later that evening, they both reappeared wearing matching blue and white polka-dot dresses and grinning ear-to-ear.

Healing Rain

One of the hardest parts of surgery is the day before. As with most surgeries, I was restricted to a clear liquid diet and I will probably never eat Jell-O or broth again. Also, because this surgery involved opening my mid-section and the possibility that the cancer may have invaded the bowels, I got to do a cleansing. As is most July days in Northern Virginia, a swampy area, the weather was hot and humid. But, I spent most of the day on the front porch anyway. When it came time for the cleansing, I began drinking the bottle of syrupy stuff and awaited its effects. However, I had apparently not read all the directions and I finished the entire bottle in less than an hour.

Within fifteen minutes it decided to make its way out in the opposite direction and I threw up everything, including the green Jell-O I had eaten earlier—yuck. We called the doctor and I was terrified that I would have to do it all over again. Fortunately, he told me to take a massive amount of laxatives instead, which was much easier. The results were not though.

I resumed my porch sitting and noted that a rainstorm had come in and the sky was completely overcast—except right over my house. From my porch I could see a parting of the clouds and pink skies. I had my iPad with me and started listening to one of my favorite Michael W. Smith songs—Healing Rain. And as the rain came down, the laxatives began to work and I found myself spending the rest of the evening and much of the night in the bathroom. Okay, for most of you this is too much information. But there was some magic in that night too. My oldest daughter, who is a mommy to two and one on the way, got stuck with the sh&*(*&(ty jobs ... she sat just outside the open bathroom door and sang to me and talked to me and we listened to Healing Rain over and over again. Being a mommy herself, she was not grossed out (much) by all the fun stuff I was going through and I so appreciated her company and diversions.

We Got It All

I had not been in an operating room since I was six years old and had a tonsillectomy, twice—but that's another story. On the morning of Aug 2, my husband and all of my children piled into my car and off we went to the hospital. We hit some traffic on the way and my husband started to get worried until I reminded him that they weren't going to start the operation without me. We sang songs and laughed and it was almost as if we were on a car trip that was many of our vacations. We were starting on a new journey.

I had no clue what having surgery would be like. The closest I could anticipate was what I'd seen on the TV show *Grey's Anatomy*—which I mentioned to the people in the operating room just before I fell asleep. As the nurses began to get me dressed for the occasion and prepared me for what was to come, and as Dr. K began to do his job, and the anesthesiologist made sure I stayed asleep, and the radiologist helped guide Dr. K through the mess that was my belly—around fifteen of my closest family members gathered in the waiting room.

My husband, my pastor, my parents, my sister, my children, my mother-in-law, and both of my brothers-in-law, all held each other and prayed that I would be all right. The surgery was scheduled for 3-4 hours—maybe longer if the cancer had invaded my bowels, which was expected. But in less than 3 hours Dr. K appeared in the waiting room. He greeted each member of my entourage, shaking everyone's hand and looking them all in the eye as he told them that he had gotten it all. He removed a 5-lb tumor, performed a full hysterectomy, removed 12 lymph nodes, and took biopsies of all surrounding organs and tissues.

Within an hour I was awake and wheeled into my room where my mother, my husband, my children, and my son's girlfriend Diane welcomed me. Be careful who you let into your room while you're under the influence of narcotics. As I looked around the room and saw all the smiling faces, the only person I acknowledged was Diane. I don't know why, but it's kind of funny. They told me what Dr. K had said, but it didn't really phase me because that was exactly what I had expected.

The next morning Dr. K came into my room and told me the same things that he had told my family the day before. But there was a change. Previously, Dr. K had guarded his words. He watched my eyes whenever he told me anything and made sure I understood what he was saying. But he never said more than what he thought I was ready to hear. That morning, he told me everything and he was not at all guarded. I have said before that I trust this man and I know that he is doing 100% of what he can to fix me. In that moment as our eyes met and he told me, "We Got It All", I knew he was right. I still had a battle to fight. Since I was Stage III-C, and it was expected that the cancer was in the lymphatic system—we still had to face the chemo-therapy and the possibility that the cancer could be other places that were not explored during that surgery. I knew there would be more to come, but at that moment I trusted Dr. K and I knew that I would be ok.

Now You See It, Now You Don't

A couple of weeks after surgery, I received a call from Dr K. We talked for several minutes about how I was doing, my activity and pain levels, and then he said, "I have your pathology results back and I'm very surprised—it's good news." He went on to tell me that he had taken biopsies of the 12 lymph nodes he had removed as well as many other biopsies of surrounding organs and multiple sections of my abdominal wall. The pathology report showed that everything, with the exception of the tumor that had been my left ovary, was absent of cancer cells. The cancer had been restricted to just the 5-lb. tumor and had not found its way into any other organs or the lymphatic system. He further told me that I was officially reduced from Stage III-C to Stage I-A. I would still need to do chemotherapy because the type of cancer was a very aggressive kind and the chance of recurrence was relatively high without treatment and significantly reduced with treatment (note—I have not included any statistics). He expected that the number of treatments would be less than he had previously anticipated.

I immediately called my husband who was at the grocery store and told him that I had news from Dr. K. After I told him what the doctor had said, he was quiet for a few moments. I asked him if he was okay. He said, "I'm just trying to hold it together—I am in public you know." And then we both laughed. I called each of my children who, as it turned out, were all serving God in one way or another. The first one I reached was my son who was running the soundboard for the rehearsal for the Navy Choir for that week's Sunday service. I asked him to hold the phone next to the speaker for a minute so I could hear the music and it was beautiful. The next was my oldest daughter who stepped out of church, where her husband was preaching his first sermon to the youth, to take my call. And my middle daughter was returning from taking a group of youth from our church on a rafting trip.

I know that not every prognosis changes as dramatically positively as mine did. I have met many women who have had the opposite happen, and many who have had recurrences. I know just how blessed I am and I hold on to that every day.

Joy Tears are Different from Sad Tears

Throughout this journey we have all cried many different kinds of tears. Shock tears in those first few days, scared tears, angry tears, frustrated tears, pain tears, but the best tears are the joy tears. I have shared different segments of this book with my family as I was writing it. One day, my husband overheard me reading a section to my daughter. I thought it might be something that would apply to a situation she was dealing with. I looked up and saw tears streaming down my husband's face. I stopped and said, "Are you okay?" He replied, "Joy tears are different than sad tears—they don't sting."

For years I associated joy tears with "mommy moments." My kids would look at me from the stage as they were singing or performing in a play, or as they did something spectacular (like not falling down) on a sports field, or brought home a good grade or any other number of childhood accomplishments. And, if my eyes were welling up (which they did a lot)—they'd know mom was having a "mommy moment." Joy moments, mommy moments, daddy moments, just that something that says "it is good." Those are the things that make everything else worth it.

Why Am I in This Office

My baby boy finished Navy basic training and had just completed his first school at Great Lakes Naval Base just north of Chicago. He had not yet received orders for his next school. It was likely the orders would be several months out and then another several months before he actually transferred to wherever he would be sent. During this time he was considered a *SNUFI*, which stands for Student Not Undergoing Formal Instruction. SNUFI's would line up in the morning to volunteer for various jobs around the base. One morning, a call came out for a SNUFI in my son's rating (Fire Control), so he volunteered and was escorted to an office. I mentioned earlier that my son has the gift of dyslexia, which gives him an advantage in many areas of his life. Office work is not one of those areas. He was also told that he would be in that job for the duration of his SNUFI—which could be as many as 4-6 months. He was confused and frustrated and kept asking, "Why am I in this office?" This happened about two weeks before he came home on leave, the day before my diagnosis. He was able to be home until just a few days after surgery.

The following Monday, he returned to his base and to his office job. The very next day, someone from a neighboring office came into his office and asked if anyone wanted orders to a 10-month school in Virginia, leaving the following week. Cody immediately volunteered and after reviewing the orders he learned that it was his first choice of school, that he would arrive just before my birthday, which was about ten days later, and that he would be only about an hour and a half from home for the next ten months. Did my wonderful son call me and tell me his good news ... No. He told everyone else and swore them to complete secrecy.

The Friday before my birthday, my middle daughter informed me that she was flying to Tennessee to visit some friends. On Sunday, I took her to the airport. Being the caring mother I am, I always track my children as they travel. Ordinarily, I would have to know all their flight information and I would track the flight to know when it took off and landed. But, for some reason, I didn't even ask this time. And where did my daughter go? Not to Tennessee! She flew to Chicago and met Cody, who had bought her the ticket. Then they got in his car and drove to Tennessee, as she really did want to visit some friends. Then they drove to southern Virginia to visit their sister for a day and night.

Around noon on my birthday, as I was sitting on my front porch (on a conference call with my boss and several other work "friends"), my dad returned from "looking at new cars." I had my back to the driveway and did not see him arrive, and as I turned around, my son was climbing the front steps. My first reaction was that my dad had picked him up from the airport to surprise me for my birthday (which was exactly what they wanted me to think). Shortly after that, my daughter arrived—driving my son's car—with his bicycle strapped to the back and all of his *stuff* piled in the trunk and backseat. I didn't know what to make of this. As she climbed the steps to the porch, she handed me a manila envelope and said, "Hmm, wonder what this could be". I opened the envelope, and my son pointed out the details of his orders to Dahlgren, VA (1½ hours from my home) and that he was to be stationed there for at least ten months. They definitely got me. It was the absolute best birthday present I could ever have wanted.

We Kicked Cancer's Butt—
The Party

My birthday was 3½ weeks after surgery and one week after I received my pathology results and upgraded prognosis. So I decided for the first time—maybe ever—to throw myself a party. I called our favorite restaurant. It is the only restaurant my husband and I ever go to now, because if we ever go anywhere else— we always ask ourselves, why we ever go anywhere else. This restaurant is built in a series of converted farm buildings, including a two-story main house, and a huge barn. Each room has a different theme, ranging from a bar area intended for mingling singles, to the 60-table barn for family dining, the Washington room and the Racing room where white table cloths adorn intimately arranged tables that provide for more private dining, and the Audubon room that has huge leather chairs that I can't sit in because I can't reach the table. The food is always wonderful and the menu maintains several staples, but changes enough to allow for plenty of variety—even when we go 3 or 4 times a month.

The main house area of the restaurant offers two upstairs dining rooms that can be reserved for private parties. I called and booked one of the rooms and began planning the menu. When the party planner asked me the occasion for the party, I told her it was my birthday—but that I was really celebrating *kicking cancer's butt*. I had not started chemo yet, but given that the pathology report showed that the cancer was only in the tumor and it was gone, my doctor had told me that I was already essentially cancer-free. I knew they posted signs for private parties and told her that we could just say "Tania's Birthday Party" on those signs. But she said, "I think we should call it what it is." When we arrived at the restaurant we were greeted by a sign that said "We Kicked Cancer's Butt and Tania's Birthday Party" and an arrow pointing upstairs. The menus were titled the same way. We enjoyed a lovely evening with great food and 20 of our closest friends and family.

Angels on My Shoulders

My sister makes jewelry. It is not her full-time job, though she sometimes wishes it were; it is her therapy. She makes enough money selling her creations to support her habit. She also gives away a lot of her proceeds by sharing her jewelry creations with me. She will often make a pair of earrings or a necklace, post its picture on her Facebook page, and then tag me if it's something she thinks I may like. One Saturday afternoon, she posted a picture of "angel" earrings.

They were pretty little beads interspersed with wings and a halo on top. I immediately "liked" them, which is the code for—"Yes, I want these." The next morning was the first Sunday after surgery that I felt able to go to church and I thought to myself, Oh, I'll wear those lovely angel earrings. I searched my dresser, I searched the bathroom, I searched the kitchen counter and could not find the earrings anywhere. Then I realized she hadn't actually given them to me yet. I'd just seen them on the computer the night before. It was several days later that I met my sister for yogurt and she handed me the pretty little angel earrings. Of course I had to share my Sunday story with her and we had a good laugh.

Several days later, I had an idea. I called my sister and asked if she could make similar earrings, but with teal colored beads, for Ovarian Cancer awareness. "Of course," she said. But, she didn't make just one pair. She made me ten pair and has made several more since. I've kept some of them so that I can trade out, and always wear angels on my shoulders. I've also given away several pairs to friends. One day, I took some to my chemo treatment with me and gave them to several of my new friends. Every one of them changed out whatever earrings they were wearing and have worn them to every treatment since. I am so thankful for my sister and being able to share her gift. She has also made several pair with pink beads for Breast Cancer and they are both big sellers at her shows—getting the word out on both diseases, and spreading angels all over the world.

Around the World in 330 days

My middle daughter has been drawn to serving others and missionary work for a long time. She has given up her school breaks and summers to do God's work in Virginia, New Jersey, California, and Tennessee. Her story is hers to tell, but a piece of her story is a big part of my journey with cancer. Kacie signed up for The World Race in January, nearly eight months before my diagnosis. The World Race is an 11-month, 11-country mission. She had been raising funds and collecting the various supplies she would need. In July (at the time of my diagnosis) she was nearly fully funded, had completed her training camp, and only needed a few more shots and supplies to be ready to go. She had not received her launch date, but was expecting to leave in early September.

When I received my diagnosis, she thought that meant she couldn't or shouldn't go on with her plans. In the early days, none of us knew how it would affect any future plans we had. I told her early on we didn't know enough to make any decisions and I didn't want her to change her plans just yet. There were others in my family who disagreed and thought she needed to plan to stay home, but much of this was based on their fears for her planned trip rather than my need for her to be home. I continued to tell her that whatever was supposed to happen would make itself evident. God would tell her if she should go or not.

Once the pathology report came back, and it appeared that I was already cancer-free and just had to go through the ugliness of chemo, I encouraged Kacie to continue with her plans. I knew how important it was to her. I knew that she would go eventually. The selfish part of me wanted her to go, so she would come back sooner. I knew it would be hard on both of us. Kacie had been living at home and working at the same office as I for nearly a year. We had become more than mother-daughter or housemates, we had become friends.

As it came time to make the go/no-go decision, and especially when her brother was stationed so close to home and she knew he'd be nearby to be here for me when or if I needed him, it was clear that she needed to go. Before she left, Kacie made joy cards and put them in envelopes to be opened the day of each of my chemo treatments. These joy cards reminded me of the little things that are so important. Just the act of making the cards was a joy in itself, and the messages included on each card are constant reminders of the beauty that is my baby girl and how God is working in her life.

Kacie left two days before my first treatment. She has spent a month each in Romania, Moldova, Nepal, and India. As I write this, she is on her way to Africa where she will spend several months in various countries and then back to Asia and Europe before she comes home in August. She has lived in conditions that many of us could never imagine. She has witnessed God's miracles in the poorest regions of the world. She has worked in a cancer hospital. She has loved special-needs children in a place where others see them as cursed. She has also helped a teammate deal with her father's cancer diagnosis. She sent me a message in what was her middle of the night and asked me to pray immediately because she knew God would hear my prayer for her friend and her friend's father. I told her that this was another blessing. At first, she didn't understand. But then I explained that God prepared her to be able to help her friend by seeing her through my diagnosis and all that she went through in those early days.

Kacie has not been here for my chemo treatments, or the recovery periods after each. She has not been here for birthdays, Thanksgiving, Christmas, my aunt's funeral, or the everyday moments. She is missed terribly, and many times has wanted to be home. She is doing what she is meant to do and is making a difference and collecting blessings and joys of her own.

She does not have a phone and relies on spotty Internet connections for limited communication. In spite of these limitations, we have had some wonderful joy moments together. She was the first to tell me I was beautiful without hair on one of our video calls just a few days after my hair began falling out. I have helped her process some of her experiences and been a voice outside of her circumstances to help her see the joys that are sometimes hidden. Neither of us would trade this experience for her.

To Know or Not to Know

The most shocking day, second only to diagnosis day, was Chemo-Training day. My mother, my husband and I spent over two hours with one of the chemo nurses, learning everything there was to know about chemo. She provided a packet detailing every possible side-effect, how to potentially prevent them and what to do if/when they happened. We went through pages and pages of nastiness. It was overwhelming and it was the first time that chemo became a reality to me. It was also the same day that the DC area experienced a major earthquake. I was driving home on I-66—which is a fairly bumpy road anyway—and I remember thinking that the road was in especially bad shape. I didn't know there'd been an earthquake until I got home. My earth was quaked that day and it took me several hours of alone time to decompress.

Having been through chemo now, and talking with many other chemo patients, I can tell you that nobody has all of the side-effects, so even though they tell you about all of them that doesn't mean you will experience them all. Modern medicine has all but eliminated the nausea and upchucking typically associated with most chemo-therapy drugs. This is accomplished through a variety of steroids and anti-nausea medicines. I was amused to discover that my daughter was prescribed two of the same anti-nausea medicines for her morning sickness. Don't hesitate to take advantage of these drugs. They do help. I have experienced mild nausea that quickly disappeared within a few minutes of taking the drugs. One night I had left my medicine downstairs and as my husband was already snoring, I thought I'd just wish the nausea away. That didn't work ... so take the drugs.

The anticipation of the side-effects is worse than the experience. After my first treatment I kept reviewing all the possible side effects in my head and as the days passed, I imagined the onset of every single one of them. But they didn't all materialize. During and after the first treatment, each person learns which things will affect them and which likely will not. The hard part is that the side-effects are cumulative, so they do get worse with each treatment. But you also learn to cope better each time.

I have a friend who went through chemotherapy several years ago. She was not given any chemo training. She had lots of medical-ease literature, but it was difficult to understand. When she began to experience various side-effects, she was not sure if it was normal or not.

In retrospect, it is better to be informed, but don't let information overwhelm you. Recognize that just like every other part of this experience, each person will react to the chemo drugs differently and will experience a unique set of side-effects to varying degrees. Know what might happen and know how you should react, what medicines or other treatments to use, but don't let it freak you out. It's all a part of the journey.

She Needs a Mommy Very Badly

"Hook" was one of our favorite movies when my children were little. I remember it was the first movie that we saw in the theater, and watched for the video (VHS at the time) to come out so we could watch it again and again. There are two lines that have resonated with me throughout this journey. One of them was when Peter Pan removed Capt. Hook's wig to reveal his balding head with spotty white strands. Hook says, "Give a man some dignity." This is the line I used when I donned my hats as my hair got thinner and thinner. But that's not what this segment is about. The second line is spoken as Peter Pan is rescuing his children, Maggie tells Capt. Hook "You need a mommy very badly." She was referencing his bad manners and poor disposition. But, it hit home during my journey.

My mother is a saint. She does anything for anyone and gets very little thanks. The day of my diagnosis I told her that she might need to pack a bigger suitcase for her upcoming visit to my house. This was because I knew that if I asked her to, she would stay with me for as long as I needed her. And she did.

Mommys are a special breed, but mine is even more unique. She put her life completely on hold for nearly four months for me. She helped me shower, helped me dress, cooked for me, made me eat, made sure I took all the medicine I was supposed to take on time, and put up with my bad attitude from time to time. She laughed with me and even screamed with me as I learned to "scream away coughs."

Remember that my first known ailment was an allergy to my daughter's pet rabbit. Said rabbit was still a part of my world right after surgery. Anyone who has had any kind of abdominal surgery knows that coughing is not a fun event. I still had the cough, but learned that if I screamed it forced air through my lungs, chest, and throat, and most of the time the cough would subside without the usual painful explosion.

My mom napped with me and sometimes for me. She fixed all sorts of foods in an effort to find something that would taste good. She washed my sheets and made my bed. She watched movies with me. She sat on the porch with me. She took me to my doctor appointments and shopping when I was up to it. She helped me finish a quilt I had been working on and made curtains for my bathroom.

And she took me to my first chemo appointment that happened to be on her birthday. I count as one of my greatest joys my mom.

Party in the Chemo Room ...

Nurses in general are a special type of people, but chemo nurses are in a class by themselves. Nurses give so much of themselves to people who are hurting and are often not nearly as grateful as we should be. Nurses work hard long hours on their feet all day. Chemo nurses have a really hard job. They are working with people who are going through some of the worst experiences in their lives. Their patients are dealing with so much, and these nurses are poisoning them to make them better. By the way, who was the first person who volunteered to be poisoned in order to get better?

The nurses at my doctor's infusion clinic are the best in the world. From the first day of chemo training until the day I "graduated" from chemo, they were angels. I could call anytime with any question and they would always call me back with a smile in their voice. When they called to tell me that my blood counts were down so low that I needed to be on house-arrest, they did it in a way that I didn't worry and knew exactly what I needed to do.

On chemo days, they made the atmosphere party-like. The room was full of snacks, laughter, hugs and reassurance. These nurses were able to explain some things in ways that the doctors just can't. I saw them hold hands with women who were crying. I saw them hug everyone who came in and call them by name. And, in spite of the environment and what was really happening (again the poison), they made the room a happy place to be.

Mexi-Slop vs. The Food Network

One of the probable side-effects of chemo-therapy is what I call "metal mouth." Everything has a metallic taste and smell. Combining this with a need to eat five or six times a day is challenging. Nothing tastes good, and most foods are just downright nasty. Early on, I started trying to think of foods or flavors that could break through the metal, but not upset my stomach.

One night I gave my mom a list of ingredients. I'm not sure where they came from, but it just sounded like it would work. I asked for ground beef, fresh tomatoes, corn, green peppers, salt and pepper, and a little taco seasoning. She served this with a flour tortilla to sop up the juices. Since this was a made-up recipe, we decided to call it "Mexi-slop."

Daytime TV is just plain awful, but I have discovered a new channel that I previously thought was an indulgence my busy lifestyle did not allow—"The Food Network." This channel is dangerous; I get so many ideas for foods that have a lot of flavor. I am constantly sending my husband to the grocery store to buy obscure ingredients that are hard to find. I have discovered many new foods that taste great, and I have made lots of new dishes I never knew I could make, including coconut shrimp with pineapple (see

"What Does Your Blood Say About You"), four different types of egg rolls, cinnamon rolls, gnocchi with veggies and thyme, beef wellington, flavorful meatloafs, and we had the best Thanksgiving turkey ever thanks to "The Barefoot Contessa." These cooking shows have given us lots of ideas for many different flavors that cut through the metal mouth and make eating fun again.

Do You Want To Lie Down Now, or Do You Want To Wait Until You Reach the Bed

One of the benefits that my company provides is a nurse advocate to help patients traverse "catastrophic illnesses." I had a hard time admitting that my diagnosis constituted a catastrophic anything, but I was thrilled with my new friend Kathy. She came to my home a few weeks after surgery and before chemo began to get to know me and learn more about my diagnosis and prognosis. And after that she called every week to check up on me and see what she could do to help me understand anything my doctor had told me or help with symptoms I was experiencing. She was also available to work with my doctors and nurses if I needed that help. It is a wonderful benefit.

The week following my first treatment, Kathy called to see how I was managing and what symptoms I was experiencing. We talked about the metal mouth, which was beginning to subside, and the neuropathy, which wasn't too bad. Then I mentioned that I got tired quickly, but said, "It's ok, I'm pushing through it." Kathy chuckled and said, "Oh no, Miss Tania, this is not the kind of fatigue you push through. If you keep trying that your body is going to ask you, 'Do you want to lie down now, or do you want to wait until you reach the bed?'" This was very liberating.

Several of the websites and pamphlets I had read said it was important to do some moderate exercise to help with the fatigue. This is true; I have definitely found that if I stay put too long I end up feeling worse than when I am up moving around more. But, when the fatigue takes over, let it. I set daily goals for exercise (starting with up and down the stairs once a day—followed by a walk to the mailbox the next day—ten minutes on the treadmill—maybe a Wii game of bowling or golf—and eventually a walk to the end of my neighborhood (about a mile but not until the 2nd or 3rd week after treatment). After the first few treatments, I knew what my limits were and I was so thankful that Kathy had given me permission to give in and lie down.

One other thing to note about chemo induced fatigue. Once you have reached your fatigue point for the day, you're done. Sometimes it's 10 am, sometimes it's 7 pm. But it's not something where you can take a little rest and be rejuvenated, so plan your days accordingly. I learned that if I needed to get something at all strenuous done (such as running errands), it should be in the morning and that I would likely be done for the day.

Another good way to ease the fatigue is to take advantage of the motorized carts that many stores have. Be sure to wipe the handles with sanitizing wipes. Also, take

someone with you to unplug and plug in the carts because they're usually plugged into obscure outlets. More importantly, you want someone you can race down the aisles ☺. These carts are a lot of fun and will help you get more shopping done without getting too tired. One day while checking out at my local grocery store, an elderly lady tapped me on the shoulder and leaned down and said, "Oh, I've always wanted to ride on one of those, is it fun?" I told her it was great fun and that if she really wanted to have a good time to ride the ones at Costco because the aisles were wider and the carts had more power than most so you could really go fast.

Seeing the world from a motorized cart or any kind of wheelchair gave me a whole new perspective. Not so much about what I could see, but what I observed in others. Most people would not make eye-contact with me when I was in the chair. Many would seem to look right through me. I truly came to appreciate the people who would stop and say hello, the checkout girl who talked to me just the same as she would have had I had been her height, the man who offered to reach something on a high shelf—which he would likely have needed to reach for me if I were standing my full 5'2", and the people who would just smile as they passed by. That was my normal and the joy that I held on to instead of all those who either wouldn't look at all, or who wore a pity face. Don't pity those who appear less fortunate than you, but if you do—don't let them see it.

What Does Your Blood Say About You

Regular blood tests are an important part of the chemo-therapy experience. A doctor once described me as a turnip, referencing the phrase "you can't get blood from a turnip" because I have small, deep veins that are hard to reach. So, I was not at all happy about the prospect of weekly blood tests. While in the hospital a phlebotomist visited my room for a routine blood test and after she poked me the third time to no avail I insisted that she go find someone who knew what she was doing. I ended up with a bruise that covered the entire underside of my arm and another on my hand that lasted well over a month. A good phlebotomist should only need to poke you once.

Regular blood tests will tell you and your doctor how well you are tolerating the chemo treatments. You may feel perfectly fine, but your blood may say something different. Chemo treatments and recovery are cyclical. Blood counts are typically affected during the mid-point of your recovery period, after you've started to feel a little better.

Chemo can affect your red blood counts and hemoglobin. Red blood cells carry oxygen throughout your body and when they are low you are anemic, which may cause you to feel more tired or dizzy. Increasing your iron intake through diet is the best way to increase your hemoglobin, but if your red cells drop too low a transfusion may be necessary. Don't take iron supplements unless your doctor prescribes them because they can cause constipation which is already another side-effect that you want to avoid. My hemoglobin dropped below normal a few times, but not dangerously so. By the way, another tasty dietary addition is pizza. If your hemoglobin is low and your white count is down, preventing you from eating the green leafy veggies that can increase your iron levels, try pizza. Pizza dough is enriched with iron and meats such as pepperoni and sausage are high in iron.

Chemo can also affect your platelets, which may make you at more risk for bleeding. If this happens you're more apt to bruise easily and any other type of bleeding from injury or otherwise may take longer to clot. In the United States there is no approved or recommended treatment for low platelets other than a transfusion. However, a wonderful nurse friend of mine was aware of a treatment that is recommended in other countries and one which she had personally experienced success. Adding fresh pineapple to your diet can increase platelets. I have recommended this to several chemo friends who were suffering from low platelets that prevented them from having treatments on time, and for at least two of them it worked. Several times, my platelets dropped and I immediately ate more pineapple and the counts went back up. I cannot medically say that they are related, but hey pineapple tastes good anyway.

The blood count that affected me the most was my white blood count. Usually about ten days after my treatment, my white counts would drop. More importantly, my absolute Neutrophils dropped to dangerous levels. Absolute Neutrophils are the white blood cells that are mature enough to fight off infections. My ANC counts would typically go so low that I was put on house arrest: stay away from anyone who might be sick, use lots of hand sanitizer and wash my hands and face often, stop eating any fresh fruits or veggies that could not be fully cooked or peeled, fully cook all meats, don't touch raw meats, stay away from pets, and a whole slew of other precautions to keep from being exposed to anything that may cause an infection. Usually this happened just about the time I was getting over the fatigue and bloating and other uncomfortable symptoms and was ready to face the world again. Fortunately, my counts always came back up again in time for the next treatment. One of my chemo friends experienced such a drop in her ANC that she ended up with a bad infection and was hospitalized for several days. She had to take shots the day after each subsequent chemo treatment. These shots helped stimulate her bone marrow and made it so that she was healthy enough to receive her treatments on time.

 One day I found a package in the mail from my boss. I laughed for ten minutes when I opened it to find little stuffed white blood cells in a

6" Petri-dish. Once I had stopped laughing enough to catch my breath, I called him to thank him and he said, "I heard you could use some extras."

The most important blood test for those experiencing Ovarian Cancer is the CA-125. This test measures tumor cells in your body. The normal range for the CA-125 is between 0 and 34. The day of my diagnosis, my reading was 509. After surgery the count went down to 99. After each treatment I would get a new reading. Ideally, the count gets within normal range and stays at whatever your baseline should be. My first reading after the first treatment was 19. The next reading was 34. This was scary, until I learned that each lab tests a little differently and I had been to two different labs for these tests. From then on I stayed with just one lab (and a phlebotomist who hit the vein the first time every time). Subsequent tests showed a continuous downward slope which was good, but I never established a consistent reading or baseline. More about that in The End is In Sight—Maybe.

Today my doctor has called my baseline 20 and we will continue to monitor this count every 3 months for the next 2 years. It will likely move around a little, but the goal is to keep it in normal range without an upward trend. It is wonderful that this test exists, because it can diagnose potential tumor cells and indicate the need for additional tests before cancer is too advanced. One may wonder why this test is not part of normal annual screening for women. The reason is that it can have false positives, which might necessitate additional tests to rule out cancer, such as ultra-sounds and CT scans. The insurance industry is not willing to mandate this test because the increase in these expensive follow-on tests is beyond what they're willing to pay. However, if you are experiencing any of the symptoms that I described previously, which could indicate possible Ovarian Cancer—insist on this test. If you test in the normal range, all is good. Studies show that there are not normally false negatives.

I have proven that you can get blood out of a turnip and it has a lot to say.

How to Save a Bundle on Shampoo and Shave Cream

I have never considered myself a vain person. Though I don't stay in sweats or pajamas all day long, the first criteria for my choice of clothing is comfort. I do not typically wear much, if any, make-up. My back injury made high heels a near impossibility, so they've never been part of my wardrobe. So, why would my first concern with chemo be hair-loss? I have always had thick, somewhat wavy hair. It has not been shorter than shoulder length since I was two. I am not defined by my hair, but losing it has been one of the hardest parts of the journey.

Just before my first treatment, I visited my hairdresser who gave me my first *short* haircut ever. Kacie was with me and I did cry a little. It only took a couple of days to realize how much easier short hair was to care for. A quick shampoo and comb and I was good to go. My doctor wrote me a prescription for a "cranial prosthesis"—a wig. The American Cancer Society gives out free wigs. I tried on several wigs of various lengths and styles. The natural hair wigs have to be washed and styled. The synthetic wigs can melt in the kitchen. Both kinds were itchy and hot. Ultimately, I decided not to get a wig.

About ten days after my first treatment, this shorter hair began to fall out. My scalp was achy and itchy, and it seemed every time I turned around I was finding piles of hair. For about a week, I would go outside and comb out my hair several times a day and leave a pile. One night I decided to take a bath and soak my head. It felt great. Afterwards the tub looked as if Big Foot or Chewbacca had been bathing. We put a screen in the drain and my wonderful husband cleaned the tub.

Several websites recommended shaving my head to take control of the situation. I didn't lose all my hair after the first treatment, so I decided to wait and see what would happen. About ten days after each subsequent treatment I would begin losing a little more hair. I never lost all of it, but enough that I am not comfortable without a hat outside of my house or with anyone other than my immediate family. My hairdresser *trimmed* the remaining hair twice. Most of what remains is white and it is about ¼ inch long. I look like an old marine sergeant.

Perhaps the harder part was the losing of my eyelashes and eyebrows. Did you know that eyebrows keep water from running into your eyes? I tried drawing them on once, but they looked quite ridiculous.

There are, however, quite a few advantages to this hair loss. I have not had to shave my legs for over five months. Showers are significantly shorter. I have not had to buy shampoo, conditioner, or shaving cream. The hair loss is not discriminatory. It happens everywhere. One of the lesser discussed features is the bikini wax, sans wax.

When all is said and done, it's just hair. It will grow back and has already started. My head will be a fresh clean slate. I can do whatever I want, whatever color, whatever style. One thing I have decided is to keep it short.

Chemo-Caps and Camaraderie

My little sister is an angel in disguise. I've already written about her angel earrings, but she also played a huge part in my acceptance of the hair loss. The day I got my short haircut, and shopped for wigs, she brought over a "present." Inside were twenty different "chemo-caps" in varying styles, fabrics, weights. Some were embroidered by her sister-in-law, some were fancy, some were simple and they were all wonderful.

That weekend would be the last weekend all my kids were together for a year, so I asked to take a family picture. We took several, but the best was when someone suggested that we all try on some of my new caps. Even my two grandchildren got in on the fun, both showing their profiles in the photo below.

I have made several more caps and given several away. I now have some with *bling*, Christmas caps, and am currently working on some that will help usher in spring in style. The caps are so much more fun to play with than blow dryers and curling irons.

Where'd the Floor Go

My back injury resulted in some nerve damage that manifests itself in numbness or aches in my left leg and right foot. So, I had some experience with neuropathy. Chemo-induced neuropathy was different though. I experienced two types. During the first week after treatment, my major muscles—thighs, abdomen and sometimes biceps and back—ached and were very weak. There were several days after each treatment when I could not walk up the stairs, but had to crawl because I could not trust my legs to hold me up. The weakness passed after a couple of days, but the achiness persisted until the second week.

The second and more common type of neuropathy affected my fingers and toes. It didn't really affect me much after the first treatment, so I thought it might be one of the side-effects I would miss. About 7-10 days after each subsequent treatment I noticed that the floor got softer and softer until it just wasn't there anymore. The numbness began at the tips of my fingers and toes and with each treatment it progressed a little further up my hands and feet. Days 14-18 my feet felt like hobbit feet. Usually the symptoms subsided before the next treatment. But, they never really went away completely after the 5th or 6th treatments. Neuropathy is one of the side-effects that can linger several months or longer after chemo is over.

The End is In Sight—Maybe

When my pathology results came back, Dr K told me that we'd do fewer treatments than the six to eight he'd originally envisioned. The protocol for my type of cancer was four to six treatments. Dr K said studies showed that typically six was no better than four and so he prescribed four treatments. The first was on my mother's birthday and the last was scheduled for my late sister's birthday. If all went well, I'd be done well before Thanksgiving and would enjoy a cancer-free, treatment-free Christmas.

After my third treatment, my CA-125 blood test had not yet stabilized. I had readings of 19, 32 and 29. Although 0-34 is "normal", Dr K was looking for my baseline; that is, at least two readings the same. So, he decided to add a fifth treatment, scheduled for Dec 1. This was disappointing, but better to be safe than sorry and better to continue with the treatments rather than have to do it again.

I met many women throughout the treatments who experienced similar disappointments. Each person reacts to the treatments differently. Some cannot tolerate the treatments well and have fewer. Some cannot tolerate the dosage and have to have more treatments of less duration. Some have reactions to side effects such as blood count drops that prevent them from having their scheduled treatments and the whole process takes longer. I had no right to complain. I knew that Dr K was doing 100% of what he promised to do to fix this. So we did a fifth treatment.

Two days before my fifth treatment, Dr K got the readings from my most recent CA-125. My reading had still not stabilized and was now 24. So, he recommended that we do a sixth treatment! Another disappointment, but again better to be safe than sorry.

So, I had six chemo treatments, each lasting six hours. Thirty-six hours of partying in the chemo-room, making new friends, and doing what needed to be done to get healthy.

I'm Your Person

In several episodes of the TV show *Grey's Anatomy*, Meredith and Cristina both tell each other that they are each other's "person". This has resonated with me ever since I heard it the first time. Your *person* is the one person who is with you no matter what. This is the person who feels what you feel, happy or sad, joy or sorrow. This is the person who will accept you no matter what and be the one you can rely on.

A radical hysterectomy also means instant menopause and all the fun side-effects. The changes in hormone levels affect your moods and sometimes result in high highs and low lows, crying for no particular reason, or finding a joke funnier than it really is. When you add the mental and physical effects of chemo-therapy, the changes in your emotions can be extreme. It is important that you have at least one person in your life who is your safety net. Someone you can cry with, laugh with and who will accept you wherever you are. My sister was my person early on. She had been through so many medical trials, including a hysterectomy, and she was able to talk me off the ledge several times. As acceptance of my condition set in, and witnessing various swings in my ability to handle different situations, my husband became my person. He lets me yell when I need to yell, he cries with me, but more important he laughs with me. Our marriage has been strengthened throughout this whole process and he loves telling me "I'm your person".

The Sitting Rib Roast

I've never been a fabulous cook, though I'm getting better thanks to Food Network. But, I've usually done a pretty good job with our annual family meals at Thanksgiving and Christmas. Thanksgiving fell two weeks after my 4th treatment. I was neutropenic and not allowed to touch raw meat, such as a turkey, or eat veggies or fruits that could not be fully peeled or thoroughly cooked. I was also not allowed to go out or eat foods not prepared in my kitchen where I would know that proper care was taken.

Thankfully, I have a wonderful family who all pitched in. My son-in-law was up-to-his elbows basting and seasoning the turkey the night before and my mother-in-law and my daughter patiently prepared the meal. And our Thanksgiving dinner was wonderful. Of course, being the control-freak that I often am, I had detailed step-by-step instructions prepared with start and stop times.

Christmas came a mere four days after my sixth treatment. There was no way I was going to be able to do everything I usually did to prepare our annual standing rib roast and all the trimmings for 15 to 20 people. When I found out I would be having a sixth treatment, I told my son and my husband that I was still going to cook my annual standing rib roast dinner. My son, quick as ever, replied, "Um, no mom—you will be doing a *sitting* rib roast. You will sit and tell me what to do." Everyone pitched in and we had a wonderful meal. I really couldn't taste it that day; however the "planned-overs" were wonderful two or three days later when the metal mouth had subsided.

Chemo-Brain or Multi-tasking Streamlined

There was a time not too long ago where I could have two conference calls (one in each ear), something on the computer (or multiple somethings), and talking with someone in my office— and still manage to stay engaged with what was going on in all mediums.

Then came *chemo-brain*.

This is a very real side effect of chemo therapy. The main symptoms of chemo-brain are lack of short-term memory, inability to "find the right word", unable to concentrate, and a complete eradication of any form of multi-tasking. If the phone rings, I have to turn off the TV. I find myself playing a lot of charades to try to communicate thoughts for which no words will come. And, I forget just about everything that I don't write down. I have made more trips up and down the stairs because I have forgotten why I went one direction or the other. I saw a T-shirt I wanted to buy that said, "I have chemo-brain, what's your excuse." It is sometimes really annoying, but more often it is funny.

One book I read recommended calling your most forgetful friend, because you can talk for hours about the same thing and later have no idea what you talked about.

Streamlined tasks are actually more fun, because you have to be fully in-the-moment. Nobody or nothing gets just a piece of you. This is a side-effect that will go away. I intend to take full-advantage until it does.

Phone-A-Friend

Life is not so much about what you do, but who you do it with. There are many important people in my life. I am fortunate to have been married to the same wonderful, caring man for 28 years. I have three wonderful children and a son-in-law who I count as friends. My parents and my parents-in-law are a big part of my life. My sister and brother-in-law, and my husband's brother and his family are all within 30 minutes of my house, and while we don't see each other as often as we'd like—we're all there for each other when it counts.

It is amazing the way God sets things up for us. An important group of people in my world are the people I work with. Two and a half years before my diagnosis, my then manager told me that it was time for me to move on and do something different. This was not because I was not good at what I was doing, but in order to continue growing—I needed to do something different. Eight months before my diagnosis, the same manager offered me an opportunity to move to a different part of my company and to work for him again. It was a hard decision, but absolutely the right thing to do. Prior to this job change, I was managing 20+ people, and directed many activities that I had designed. I thought I was indispensable. In my new job, I did not have direct supervision for anyone, but helped my boss manage an organization of over 700 people. I loved my new job. I met many new people, and I got to work for the most amazing boss in the world.

When I received my diagnosis, my boss was among the first five people I told. Not only did he need to know because of the changes this was going to create in my work-ability, but he is also a wonderful friend and a part of my inner circle. I am very fortunate to work for a company that provides excellent health care and other benefits. I am even more fortunate to work for a man who sees me as a person first and then as an employee. Throughout this journey he has continued to support me and adjust my work expectations to meet my capabilities. There have been times when I could work as many as 30 hours in a week and other times when I was lucky to work four or five.

After my third treatment, the neuropathy, fatigue, and chemo-brain were especially debilitating. I was not able to concentrate on anything for more than 10 or 15 minutes. I was feeling disappointed in myself and concerned that I couldn't do the work I had agreed to do. I sent my boss an email and "confessed" that I was in worse shape than I had expected and was not going to be able to meet a deadline. The next morning, he called me and very calmly told me that my priorities were: health first, then family, and then work. I told him I was not sure what my new normal was going to be when all this was over. He said, "Are you the same person you were five years ago, or even last year? Why would you expect to be the same a year from now?

We're always changing and we are always finding our new normal." He also explained that he had a new role for me and that for the time being or until I felt up to doing more, I was going to be his "phone-a-friend." This meant that when I was up to it, I would be the person he could call to talk through ideas and if others on his team needed advice or help that he thought I could offer—they could also phone-a-friend. He also said that if I was not feeling well enough, to just say so.

We set up a task rating system. If I was up for a task, I would ping him and he would ask: 1, 2, 3, 4, or 5? A "1" task was something I could do in my sleep or with little effort. A "5" task was something that in my best condition might require several hours or days of quiet, focused work. Throughout chemo I never got above a level "3" task, but I was able to feel engaged and needed.

Just after my 4th treatment, my boss was offered an opportunity to be considered for a new job creating a whole new global organization within our company. He "phoned-a-friend" and we talked about it a lot. On the day of my 5th treatment, he began his new job. He also decided to take me along with him. So, as I am beginning my new normal—I am also beginning a new job. But as I said, it's not about what you do, but who you do it with. I am working for the best boss and looking forward to continuing to learn and grow and to find out what my new normal will be in the coming months.

I know that not everyone has the same opportunity I have had. There are many I have met on this journey who do not have the kind of health care coverage and some have been devastated by medical bills. There are others who have lost their jobs because they could not meet the demands of their workload while undergoing chemo. I know that I am extremely fortunate.

Let's Give 'em Something to Talk About

Early in this journey, I didn't want to be the subject of hallway gossip. In fact, I didn't want anyone talking about me at all. I didn't want my life to be about cancer. While I was in the hospital, a nurse came into my room and introduced herself as a nurse advocate that my doctor provided for his *cancer* patients while in the hospital. Well, the last thing I wanted at that time was to be classified as a cancer patient. It took a while for me to realize that cancer was not something to be ashamed of.

This is now a part of who I am. I am a woman, a wife, a mother, a grandmother, an employee, a friend, a church member, a singer, a pianist, a knitter, a Wii champion, a sister, a mother-in-law, a sister-in-law, a daughter, a daughter-in-law, a golfer (well I will be), a cook, a reader, a writer ... and a cancer survivor. Some of these titles I chose, some I earned, and some chose me. But regardless they are all a part of me and help in various ways to define me. And, as I take on this new role – title – curse – blessing .. I need to talk about it. It is not a secret. And, I want those around me to be comfortable talking about it. It is not something to be ashamed of. It is not something I did wrong or something that I could have or should have avoided.

Talk to me about it. It's okay!

Seasons of Life

I have lived in all four corners of the continental US. And, I have experienced every season. In Washington State—I experienced months of drizzling rain. In Florida and Georgia, I remember humidity on hot days that were like a sauna. In Rhode Island, I remember hiking from the school bus stop through several feet of cold, wet snow. And, in California it was summertime all year long. We have lived in the Washington DC area for nearly 20 years now, and while traffic is brutal, and prices for everything are through the roof, I love experiencing all four seasons.

In the summer it can get quite hot, and humid. And sometimes the snow in winter reaches several feet, but the ice storms are the worst. My favorite seasons are fall and spring.

Seasons are evident in the weather, but they are just as evident in the cycles of our lives. As I am writing this, it is winter solstice or the first day of winter. It is the shortest day of the year. But for me, it is the first day of spring because I am receiving my last chemo treatment. I know that while I will have a few icky days, in the coming weeks I can start watching for

God's blessings in new growth and rejuvenation that we see in springtime. Before too long my hair will start growing back, just like the sprouts of the crocuses and jonquils. I will see color return to my skin tone, like the grass that will turn green again. Buds on the trees offer the promise of flowers to come, followed by leaves. And I will experience an increase in energy, which will lead to a more active lifestyle. By the time the astrological springtime arrives, I will be well on my way to my new normal.

Epilogue

As I am finishing the final edits and beginning the publishing process, I am six weeks out from my last chemo. Reading and re-reading the stories in this book have been a wonderful reflection of the journey and reminder of the blessings that I've counted along the way.

I celebrated my first "day 22"—the first end of a 3-week cycle that didn't result in another treatment in five months. I celebrated the end of 2011 and the beginning of 2012 and welcome the health and energy that I know this year will bring.

Getting back to whatever my new normal will be is taking longer than I want it to take, but I can honestly say that in many ways I feel better now than I have in more than a year—maybe longer. The hair is growing back. Eyebrows are starting to be noticeable without a magnifying glass. I have more energy every day.

But, I have found myself in a bit of a funk. For more than six months, my life revolved around the next doctor's appointment or blood test. Each milestone was measured in 21-day cycles of chemo-treatments and recovery from the various side-effects. Once that was over, I found myself wondering what's next. I still have 3-month milestone check-ups, CT scans, and blood tests.

I had to remind myself that life is so much more than getting through the next hurdle. It is finding the joy moments in each day and enjoying the journey, no matter what road you are on.

Choose Joy every day. Eat the cake, or enjoy not eating it so that you can fit into those favorite jeans. Notice the red cardinal against the snowy backdrop. Find new ways to express your creativity. Learn something new. Love a lot.

Made in the USA
Charleston, SC
10 July 2012